PRINCIPLES OF
BIOGRAPHY

PRINCIPLES OF BIOGRAPHY

THE LESLIE STEPHEN LECTURE

DELIVERED IN THE SENATE HOUSE, CAMBRIDGE
ON 13 MAY 1911

BY

SIR SIDNEY LEE

Hon. D.Litt. Oxford

Cambridge :
at the University Press
1911

CAMBRIDGE
UNIVERSITY PRESS

University Printing House, Cambridge CB2 8BS, United Kingdom

Published in the United States of America by Cambridge University Press, New York

Cambridge University Press is part of the University of Cambridge.

It furthers the University's mission by disseminating knowledge in the pursuit of education, learning and research at the highest international levels of excellence.

www.cambridge.org
Information on this title: www.cambridge.org/9781107660908

First published 1911
First paperback edition 2014

A catalogue record for this publication is available from the British Library

ISBN 978-1-107-66090-8 Paperback

PRINCIPLES OF BIOGRAPHY

I

I APPRECIATE very highly the honour which the electors have done me in conferring on me the office of Leslie Stephen Lecturer in this University. A word of respectful admiration seems due to the liberality of the electors in bestowing this dignity for the second time in succession on a graduate of the sister University.

I propose to deal broadly with a very familiar ambition—the ambition to record in written words, on the printed page, the career of a man or woman. My design is to consider in the first place the essential quality of the theme which justly merits biographic effort, and in the second place to discuss the methods of presentment which are likely to serve the true purpose of biography

to best effect. Some paths which the biographer should avoid will also call for notice.
I hope to suggest causes of success or failure
in the practice of biography.

II

It is outside my scope to deal in any
detail with the biography of particular
persons. But I think I may without impro-
priety venture at the outset on a few words
about the man in whose memory this lecture-
ship has been founded, and whose name it
bears. I am conscious that I lack many
of the qualifications which my two pre-
decessors in this honourable office enjoyed.
But I believe I may without immodesty
claim one advantage in this post, which
neither of them shared with me. Leslie
Stephen was the master under whom I
served my literary apprenticeship and it was
as his pupil that I grew to be his colleague and
his friend. He gave me my earliest lessons
in the writing of biography, and in speaking
of its principles I am guided by his teaching.

I am expressing views coloured by the experience for which he trained me.

There still happily survive members of this University and literary friends in London who knew Leslie Stephen in days far earlier than those of my first acquaintance with him. Compared with the companions of his youth or early middle age I have small right to speak of him. My association with him only concerned the last twenty-one years of his life. Yet I may plead that outside the ranks of his family I owe him debts of knowledge and encouragement which have not, I think, been excelled.

Stephen belonged to a notable generation, a generation the heroes of which seem to have been cast in a larger mould than those of my own. Stephen was the affectionate disciple of Darwin, the admiring acquaintance of Tennyson, the frequent but rather critical companion of Froude, the close friend of Henry Sidgwick, of George Meredith, of James Russell Lowell. He was personally known to Browning, Ruskin,

Fitzgerald and Carlyle. With such men as these he would be the first to disclaim equality, but he belonged to their orbit.

It was Stephen's habit to depreciate himself, and to underestimate the regard in which others held him. His qualities did not make for wide popularity. He did not seek what Tennyson calls "the blare and blaze of fame." Yet he established a reputation which his greatest coevals acknowledged— a reputation which came of the virility and perspicuity of his work in ethics, in literary criticism, and above all in biography.

Justly may the University claim some share in his fame. To Cambridge Stephen owed mainly the greatest blessing of life— health, as well as a large stock of his intellectual equipment. In Stephen's case Cambridge made of a weakly boy an athletic man. His training as an undergraduate turned him into an athlete in body no less than in mind. Not that his physical health was ever obtrusively robust, but the physical exercise of his undergraduate days, in which he engaged with a wholly spontaneous zeal, clearly helped him to measure a span of life exceeding the psalmist's three score years and ten. Even more notable is the influence which this place exerted on his intellectual temper. The ideal of dry common sense, which dominated thought here in his youthful days, was his guiding star through life. He was always impatient of rhetoric, of sentimentality, of floridity in life or literature. His virtues as man and writer were somewhat of the Spartan kind. It was his life here in youth and early middle age that chiefly bred the terseness, the frankness, the dialectical adroitness which give his literary work its savour. Although he severed his connection with his University before he was forty, and though to some extent his sympathies with Cambridge afterwards decayed, its beneficent influences were never obliterated in him.

To the world at large as years advanced he seemed reserved and melancholy. I have heard him groan for hours together over the verbosity and blindness of biographers. But his seasons of depression, save in sickness, were passing moods. No man found richer solace than he in the early friendships which he formed in his University. His enthusiasm for his college while undergraduate, fellow and tutor, always kept alive happy memories, which helped to assuage sorrow, as I can testify from some evenings spent with him, when heavy domestic grief bowed down his spirit. "I love the sleepy river," he said in his last days, "not even the Alpine scenery is dearer to me."

Often a gladiator wielding unsparingly the sword of plain speech against orthodox beliefs, he dealt his strokes fairly and squarely and few of his adversaries cherished lasting resentment. Wary of enthusiasm and impatient of insincerity or incompetence, he admired without reserve all greatness in deed or thought. Every honest endeavour won his sympathy. His tenderness of heart was without any uncharitable leaven. There was always abundance of affectionate interest in those with whom he worked. Notably in his case is the style of the author the character of the man. "I think," wrote Robert Louis Stevenson, "it is always wholesome to read Leslie Stephen." The dictum is in too minor a key to sound the whole truth, but it is the unpretending sort of language which Stephen would have appreciated about himself, especially from such a quarter.

III

Biography exists to satisfy a natural instinct in man—the commemorative instinct —the universal desire to keep alive the memories of those who by character and exploits have distinguished themselves from the mass of mankind. Art, pictorial, plastic, monumental art, competes with biography in preserving memories of buried humanity. But Jacques Amyot, the great prose writer of the French Renaissance—Amyot who, by his French translation of the works of Plutarch, first made the Greek master of biography an influence on modern thought and conduct—wrote these wise words on the relative values of biography and art as means of commemorating men's characters and achievements: "There is neither picture, nor image of marble, nor arch of triumph, nor pillar, nor sumptuous sepulchre, can match the durableness of an eloquent biography, furnished with the qualities which it ought to have." "Furnished with the qualities which it ought to have"—there is the problem which we are met to face. Biography is not so imposing to the general eye as pyramids and mausoleums, statues and columns, portraits and memorial foundations, but it is the *safest* way, as Thomas Fuller wrote, to protect a memory from oblivion. Plutarch, Tacitus and Suetonius' biographical memorials of distinguished men have worn better than the more substantial tributes of art to their heroes' fame.

The aim of biography is, in general terms, to hand down to a future age the history of individual men or women, to transmit enduringly their character and exploits.

Character and exploits are for biographical purposes inseparable. Character which does not translate itself into exploit is for the biographer a mere phantasm. The exploit may range from mere talk, as in the case of Johnson, to empire-building and military conquest, as in the case of Julius Caesar or Napoleon. But character and exploit jointly constitute biographic personality. Biography aims at satisfying the commemorative instinct by exercise of its power to transmit personality.

The biographic aim implies two constant and obvious conditions. Firstly, the subject-matter, the character and achievement out of which the biography is to be woven, must be capable of moving the interest of posterity. Secondly, the manner or style of the record should be of a texture which is calculated to endure, to outlive the fashion or taste of the hour. In other words, biography depends for its successful accomplishment on the two elements of fit matter and fit manner, of fit theme and fit treatment.

Good treatment will not compensate for a bad theme, nor will a good theme compensate for bad treatment. Theme and treatment must both answer equally a call of permanent distinction. There are cases in which a good subject is found in combination with a bad form. That indeed is no uncommon experience. In the result, the commemorative instinct remains unsatisfied and biography fails to perform its function. The converse association of a bad theme with good treatment, of bad matter with good manner, is rarer, and may kindle some literary interest, although not an interest of biographic concern. For the life of a nonentity or a mediocrity, however skilfully contrived, conflicts with primary biographic principles. Unless subject-matter and style be both of a commensurate sufficiency, biography lacks "the qualities which it ought to have," the qualities which ensure permanence, the qualities which satisfy the commemorative instinct.

What constitutes fitness in a biographic

theme ? The question raises puzzling issues. The commemorative instinct which biography has to satisfy scarcely seems to obey in its habitual working any one clear immutable law. The Italian poet Ariosto imagined, with some allegorical vagueness, that at the end of every man's thread of life there hung a medal stamped with his name, and that, as Death severed life's thread with its fatal shears, Time seized the medal and dropped it into the river of Lethe. Yet a few, a very few, of the stamped medals were caught as they fell towards the waters of oblivion by swans, who carried off the medals and deposited them in a temple or museum of immortality. Ariosto's swans are biographers: by what motive are they impelled to rescue any medals of personality from the flood of forgetfulness into which they let the mass sink ?

Perhaps the old Greek definition of the fit theme of tragedy may be usefully adapted to the fit theme of biography. A fit biographic theme is, in the Aristotelian phrase, a career which is " serious, complete and of a certain

magnitude." An unfit biographic theme is
a career of trivial aim, incomplete, without
magnitude, of or below mediocrity. The
second clause in this definition, which pre-
scribes the need of completeness, offers no
ambiguity. It excludes from the scope of
biography careers of living men, careers which
are incomplete, because death withholds the
finishing touch. Death is a part of life and
no man is fit subject for biography till he is
dead. Living men have been made themes
of biography. But the choice defies the
cardinal condition of completeness. There
is usually abroad an idle curiosity about
prominent persons during their life-time. It
is not the business of biography to appease
mere inquisitiveness. Its primary business is
to be complete. The living theme can at best
be a torso, a fragment. There clings to it, too,
a savour either of the scandal or of the un-
balanced laudation which living men rarely
escape. Politicians, while they are yet active
on the political stage, are often panegyrised or
vilified by biographical partisans. The efficient

commemorative instinct, which sets little store by such panegyric or vilification, craves, before all things, the completeness which death alone assures. No man's memory can be accounted great until it has outlived his life.

At the same time there is danger in postponing indefinitely biographic commemoration in cases where it is rightly due. There are insuperable obstacles to writing the lives of men long after their relatives and associates have passed away. Even the life of Shakespeare has suffered through the long interval which separates the date of his death from the first efforts of his biographers, and there are some of Shakespeare's literary contemporaries, whose biographic commemoration has been postponed to so distant a date after their career has closed that the attempt to satisfy the just call of the commemorative instinct has altogether failed.

But the theme of biography must be far more than "complete." It must be, in addition, both "serious" and "of a certain magnitude." By seriousness we may understand the quality which stirs and firmly holds the attention of the earnest-minded.

What constitutes the needful "magnitude" in a biographic theme? It is difficult to set up a fixed standard whereby to measure the dimensions of a human action. But by way of tentative suggestion or hypothesis, the volume of a human action may be said to vary, from the biographer's point of view, with the number of times that it has been accomplished or is capable of accomplishment.

The magnitude of human action is necessarily of many degrees ; the scale ascends and descends. The production by Shakespeare of his thirty-seven plays is an action of the first magnitude, because the achievement is unique. The victory of Wellington at Waterloo is an action of great but of lesser magnitude, because deeds of like calibre have been achieved by other military commanders, and are doubtless capable, if the need arise, of accomplishment again. As we descend the scale of achievement, we reach by slow gradations the level of action which forms the terminal limit of the biographic province.

Actions, however beneficent or honourable, which are accomplished or are capable of accomplishment by many thousands of persons are actions of mediocrity, and lack the dimension which justifies the biographer's notice.

The fact that a man is a devoted husband and father, an efficient schoolmaster, an exemplary parish priest, gives him in itself no claim to biographic commemoration, because his actions, although meritorious, are practically indistinguishable from those of thousands of his fellows. It follows further that official dignities, except of the rarest and most dignified kind, give *in themselves* no claim to biographic commemoration. That a man should become a peer, a member of parliament, a lord mayor, even a professor, and attend to his duties, are actions or experiences that have been accomplished or are capable of accomplishment by too large a number of persons to render them in themselves of appreciable magnitude. At the same time office may well give a man an opportunity of distinction which he might otherwise be without; official responsibility may well lift his career to the requisite level of eminence.

In appraising the magnitude—the biographic capacity or content—of a career, one must needs guard against certain false notions —εἴδωλα or idols in Baconian terminology— which prevail widely and tend to distort the judgment. Domestic partiality, social contiguity, fortuitous clamour of the crowd—such things frequently cause mediocrity to masquerade as magnitude. The biographer has to forswear the measuring rods of the family hearth, of the hospitable board, of journalistic advertisement. A kinsman or a kinswoman, an intimate companion, is easily moved by private affection to credit undiscriminatingly a man or woman's activity with the dimensions that justify biographic commemoration. A newspaper records day by day the activities of some seeker after notoriety, until his name grows more familiar to his generation than that of Shakespeare or Nelson. Evanescent repute may very easily, through journalistic iteration, be mistaken for that which will excite the commemorative instinct hereafter.

In estimating the magnitude of human action, there is need of some workable measure or gauge which shall operate independently of mere contemporary opinion. Contemporary fame is often withheld as arbitrarily as it is bestowed. Posthumous fame at times comes into being with strange suddenness, without any contemporary heralding at all. How suggestive to the student of biography is the fact that the name and work of Gregor Mendel, the Austrian monk and biological enquirer, who died nearly thirty years ago "unwept, unhonoured and unsung," should fill ten columns of the new edition of the *Encyclopaedia Britannica*, a space in excess of that devoted to any one of the numerous heroes of science who enjoyed repute in their own lifetime. Current fame is no sure evidence of biographic fitness. The tumult and the shouting die and they may leave nothing behind which satisfies the biographic tests of completeness, seriousness and magnitude.

IV

The biographer having found his fit theme
is faced with the problem of its treatment.
His aim is to transmit personality, to satisfy
the commemorative instinct. He may learn
something of the lawful processes from a preliminary study of the processes which are un-
lawful. The main path which he should follow
may gain in clear definition if he be warned
at the outset against certain neighbouring
paths which are easily capable of leading him
astray. Biography must resolutely preserve
its independence of three imposing themes of
study, which are often seen to compete for its
control. True biography is no handmaid of
ethical instruction. Its purpose is not that
of history. It does not exist to serve biological or anthropological science. Any assist-
ance that biography renders these three great
interests—ethical, historical and scientific—
should be accidental; such aid is neither
essential nor obligatory. Biography rules a
domain of its own; it is autonomous—an
attribute with which it is not always credited.

It was an amiable tenet in the orthodox creed of an ancient biographic school, that the career destined for biographic treatment should directly teach morality, should be conspicuously virtuous. The biography should, before all else, "show virtue her own feature," or at any rate hymn her worth. Gentle Izaak Walton, like many biographers who wrote before and after him, regarded biography as "an honour due to the virtuous dead, and a lesson in magnanimity to those who shall succeed them." In Walton's demure judgment, dead men who are morally unworthy lie outside the scope of biography. It speaks well for the goodness of the world that good men have occupied more biographic pens than bad men, and that biographers have always cherished a charitable preference for benefactors over malefactors. But therein lies no proof that the merits of biography depend on its powers of edification.

It is with very large qualifications that Walton's ethical presumption can pass current. Sinners excite the commemorative

instinct as well as saints.   The careers of
both Napoleon I and Napoleon III satisfy all
conditions of the biographic theme, in spite
of their spacious infringements of moral law.
Suetonius defied no biographic principle
when he treated of Roman emperors, many
of whom were monsters of infamy. Biography
is a truthful picture of life, of life's tangled
skein, good and ill together.   Biography
prejudices its chances of success when it is
consciously designed as an ethical guide of
life.

Candour, which shall be innocent of
ethical fervour or even of ethical intention,
is a cardinal principle of right biographic
method. It is often the biographer's anxious
duty to present great achievements in near
alliance with moral failings. Coleridge was
a great poet and an illuminating thinker.
But he was deficient in the moral sense, and
justified himself for his offences by "amazing
wrigglings and self-reproaches and astonish-
ing pouring forth of unctuous twaddling."
Byron, Porson, Nelson, Parnell and many

more for whom the commemorative instinct assuredly demands biographic commemoration combined great exploits with notorious defiance of virtue.

The ethical fallacy of biography has sanctioned two evasive methods of handling such perplexing phases of life—a method of suppression and a method of extenuation. The method of suppression has found distinguished advocates. Tennyson asked "what business has the public to want to know about Byron's wildnesses? He has given them fine work and they ought to be satisfied." Here indeed we are advised, either to dispense with all biography of Byron, or only to accept a biography of him from which his "wildnesses" are excluded. The cravings of the commemorative instinct which Byron's career has already excited render both these counsels futile.

The alternative method of extenuation has been adopted by an eminent man of letters of our own day in treating of an illustrious poetic contemporary of Byron— of Shelley. Writing Shelley's life under the admiring eyes of surviving relatives, the biographer has made other people responsible for most of Shelley's flagrant errors of conduct and has credited the poet's personality with an unfailing beneficence. In view of the biographer's true goal it is difficult to speak of the whitewashing method more indulgently than of the method of suppression. The biographer is a narrator, not a moralist, and candour is the salt of his narrative. He accepts alike what clearly tells in a man's favour and what clearly tells against him. Neither omission nor partisan vindication will satisfy the primary needs of the art.

At the same time the biographer is likely to miss his aim of transmitting personality truthfully if he give more space or emphasis to a man's lapses from virtue than is proportioned to their effects on his achievement. Although he may not fill the preacher's pulpit, a touch of sympathy with human frailty, of charity for wrongdoing, will the better fit him for his task.

There is a French proverb: *Tôt ou tard,*

tout se sait—"Sooner or later everything comes to light." There is another French proverb: *Tout comprendre, c'est tout pardonner*— "To understand all is to pardon all."

Both apophthegms make appeal to the biographer, and the second is quite as relevant to his work as the first. Lives written in a hostile spirit may not be wholly untruthful. But they tend to emphasise unpleasing features and thereby give a wrongful impression. Scurrility is not candour. To pander to a love of scandal is a greater sin in a biographer than in anybody else. Lord Campbell wrote lives of lawyers, which satisfy many of the conditions of biography. But their depreciatory tone, which prompted the epigram that biography lends a new sting to death, suggests malignity and distorts the true perspective. The competent biographer may fail from want of sympathy even when his skill is not in question. Like the portrait painter who is fascinated by forbidding aspects in a sitter's countenance, he may, even without conscious intention, produce a caricature instead of a portrait.

All gradations of moral infirmity, from serious crime to mere deviation from accepted codes of good manners, will from time to time claim the biographer's notice and call for presentation in due perspective. Downright offences are not his only sources of embarrassment. Perhaps more often is he confronted with inconsistencies of conduct or opinion, with sudden changes of beliefs, religious or political, which are currently suspected of dishonesty. Defective sympathy or partisan hostility is here as harmful as any resolve to point a moral. " That conversion," says the moralist, " will always be suspected which concurs with interest." The suspicion is inevitable, but is conversion invariably dishonest? May not increase of knowledge or a greater concentration of thought on the questions at issue induce a natural and an honest process of development? Was Wordsworth a lost leader who left the revolutionary companions of his early years for the orthodox Tories just to receive a handful of silver and a bit of ribbon to stick in his coat? Was Disraeli's early abandonment of a radical

programme the act of a self-seeking ad-
venturer? Was Gladstone's unexpected
adoption of the policy of Irish Home Rule
prompted by impulses of reckless ambition,
by the hope of stealing meanly a march on
political rivals? The biographer must hold
the scales even. He must look before and
after, and close his ears to party resentments
of the hour. He must abide by the just and
generous principles which move a critical
friend's judgment. Wherever he honestly can,
a friend allows the benefit of the doubt; he
extenuates nothing, nor sets down aught in
malice. Brutus claimed that the record of
Caesar's life in the Capitol presented the
dictator's "glories wherein he was worthy" by
the side of the dictator's "offences wherein
he was unworthy." Neither were the merits
under-estimated nor were the defects over-
emphasised. Brutus's simple words suggest
the nicely adjusted scales in which the
moral blemishes of great men should be
weighed by the biographer. The aim of
biography is not the moral edification which

may flow from the survey of either vice or virtue; it is the truthful transmission of personality.

V

The pursuit by the biographer of the historian's aims may prove as disastrous as any competition with the austere aims of the moralist. The historical method is as harmful to biography as the method of moral edification. History encroaches on the biographer's province to the prejudice of his art. Bacon, in his survey of learning, carefully distinguished the "history of times" (that is, annals or chronicles) or the "history of action" (that is, histories in the accepted sense) from "lives." Bacon warns us that history sets forth the pomp of public business; while biography reveals the true and inward sources of action, tells of private no less than of public conduct, and pays as much attention to the slender wires as to the great weights that hang from them.

The distinction between history and biography lies so much on the surface that a confusion between them is barely justifiable. History may be compared to mechanics, the science which determines the power of bodies in the mass. Biography may be compared to chemistry, the science which analyses substances and resolves them into their constituent elements. The historian has to describe the aggregate movement of men and the manner in which that aggregate movement fashions political or social events and institutions. The historian has only to take into account those aspects of men's lives which affect the movements of the crowd that co-operates with them. The biographer's concern with the crowd is quite subsidiary and secondary. From the mass of mankind he draws apart those units who are in a decisive degree distinguishable from their neighbours. He submits them to minute examination, and his record of observation becomes a mirror of their exploits and character from the cradle to the grave. The historian looks at mankind through a field-glass. The biographer puts individual men under a magnifying glass.

It goes without saying that the biographer must frequently appeal for aid to the historian. An intelligent knowledge of the historical environment—of the contemporary trend of the aggregate movement of men—is indispensable to the biographer, if he would portray in fitting perspective all the operations of his unit. One cannot detach a sovereign or a statesman from the political world in which he has his being. The circumstance of politics is the scenery of the statesman's biography. But it is the art of the biographer sternly to subordinate his scenery to his actors. He must never crowd his stage with upholstery and scenic apparatus that can only distract the spectators' attention from the proper interest of the piece. If you attempt the life of Mary Queen of Scots, you miss your aim when you obscure the human interest and personal adventure, in which her career abounds, by grafting upon it an exhaustive exposition of the intricate relations of Scottish Presbyterians with Roman Catholics, or of Queen Elizabeth's tortuous foreign policy. These things are the bricks and mortar of history. Fragments of them may be needed as props in outlying portions of the biographical edifice, but even then they must be kept largely out of sight.

On these grounds I am afraid that that mass of laborious works which bears the title of " the life and times " of this or that celebrated person, calls for censure. These weighty volumes can be classed neither with right history nor with right biography. Most of them must be reckoned fruit of a mis-directed zeal. One would not wish to speak disrespectfully of the self-denying toil which has raised a mountain of stones on however sprawling a plan to a great man's memory. But when one surveys that swollen cairn *The Life of John Milton narrated in connexion with the political, ecclesiastical and literary history of his time* which occupied a great part of David Masson's long and distinguished

career, I accept in spite of the varied uses
of the majestic volumes that plaintive judgment of Carlyle :

> " Masson has hung on his Milton peg all the politics,
> which Milton, poor fellow, had never much to do with
> except to print a pamphlet or two."

Masson has hung on "his Milton peg "
not only "all the politics which Milton, poor
fellow, had never much to do with " but also
all the ecclesiastical and literary history
with which Milton had even less concern.
Biography is not a peg for anything save
the character and exploits of a man whose
career answers the tests of biographic fitness.

I should hardly be bold enough to speak
of the relations of biography and science,
and of the peril to biographic method of
bringing the two studies into too close a conjunction, had not the late Sir Francis Galton
and several living correspondents urged on
me, in my capacity of editor of *The Dictionary
of National Biography*, the general advantage
of adapting the biographic method of the

Dictionary to the needs of the scientific investigation of heredity and eugenics.

Biography, it has been argued, should serve as handmaid to this new and absorbing department of biology and anthropology. The biographer should collect, after due scrutiny, those details of genealogy, habit and physiological characteristics which may help the student of genetics to determine human types, to diagnose "variations from type," to distinguish acquired from inherited characteristics, and to arrive by such roads at a finite conception of human individuality. If biography, without deviating from its true purpose or method, can aid the scientific inquiry into the origin and development of ability or genius, all is well. But, if biographic effort is to be swayed by conditions of genetical study, if it is to inquire minutely and statistically into the distant ramifications of every great man's pedigree, with the result that undistinguished grandfathers, grandmothers, fathers, mothers, even second cousins, shall receive almost as close attention as the great man himself, then dangers may be apprehended. Whether the secret of genius will ever be solved is for the future to determine. The biographer has no call to pursue speculation on the fascinating theme.

VI

Like all branches of modern literature, biography was efficiently practised by Greece and Rome, and it is to classical tuition that the modern art is deeply indebted. It was Amyot's great French translation of Plutarch which introduced the biography of disciplined purpose to the modern world, with lasting benefit to life and literature.

Plutarch's method is in one respect peculiar to himself. He endeavours to emphasise points of character and conduct in one man by instituting a formal comparison of them with traits of similar type in another man. He writes what he calls "parallel lives" of some twenty great Greeks and Romans. Having written of Alexander the Great, he gives an account of Caesar; having written of Demosthenes, he gives an account of Cicero. In every instance he adds to his pair of lives a chapter of comparisons and contrasts. The parallel method enhances the vividness of the portraiture, but it is not the feature of his work which gives it its permanent influence. His individual themes, and his detached treatment of them, deserve chief scrutiny.

Plutarch's subjects are all leaders in politics or war. Heroes of literature and art lie outside his sphere. From the modern point of view the range is arbitrarily limited. But his limitation of theme does not prejudice the value of his example. His guiding principles of treatment are of universal application. He collects authorities in ample store. His materials included not only written books and documents, but also experience and knowledge gathered in converse with well-informed persons. He bases his narrative on contemporary evidence wherever it is accessible, but he is watchful of the lies and fables of hearsay accretions. Where two conflicting versions of one incident are at hand, he selects the one which is in closer harmony with his hero's manners and nature.

But wide as is Plutarch's field of research, he is discriminating in his choice of detail. He knows the value of perspective. He did not, he tells us, declare all things at large. At times he wrote briefly of the noblest and most notorious achievements. He preferred to concentrate his attention upon what to the unseeing eye looked insignificant— upon "a light occasion, a word or some sport." "Therein," he adds, "men's nature, dispositions and manners appear more plainly than the famous battles won, wherein are slain 10,000 men."

Personality was Plutarch's quarry. It was therefore needful for him to bring into due prominence the singularity of each human theme. His studies inevitably acquainted him with many unhappy or ungracious features in great men's lives, which asked admission to his canvas. The frailties were neither suppressed nor extenuated. Yet a sense of what he called "reverent shame" deterred him from enlarging on men's frailties beyond the needs of his art. He was a just biographer who was not distracted from his proper aim by ethical fervour or by partisanship. Nor were the purposes of history or science within his scope.

None of Plutarch's biographic principles can be ignored with impunity. Very efficiently does his example warn the biographer against two faults to which biography of more modern date has shown itself peculiarly prone—the fault of misty sentimentality or vague rhapsodizing and the fault of tediousness. The value of rhapsodical or sentimental biography is commonly overestimated when it is credited with any method at all. In a few instances an eloquent piece of literature is the outcome. But it is literature which belongs to another category than that of biography. Boccaccio's rhapsodical account of Dante is a favourable specimen of its class. We learn there much of the effect of love on youthful hearts. There is a fiery denunciation of the city of Florence for her guilt in banishing her greatest citizen. But Boccaccio's impassioned rhetoric leaves the story of Dante's life untold.

The rhapsodical or sentimental mode of biography will always have its votaries. It often makes a powerful appeal to the hearts of the ingenuous kindred of a departed relative. But the vapour of sentimentality is usually fatal to biographic light. I have already suggested how liable domestic partiality is to err in the choice of the biographic theme. It is no less harmful in ordinary conditions to biographic treatment or method. Very rarely will domestic sentiment recognize the limitations of the biographic art, or obey the cry for candour and perspective. Whether the theme be fit or no, the pen which is guided by domestic enthusiasm will, as a rule, flow to satiety with sentimental vagueness and inaccuracy. The advantage of intimate knowledge which might seem to come of a kinsman's personal

propinquity to the biographic hero counts
save in a few notable instances for very
little or for nothing. The domestic pen is
too often innocent of literary experience.
The faculty of selection and arrangement is
wanting, or is at any rate lost in the stream
of cloudy panegyric. There are tendencies
to emphasise the immaterial and to ignore
the material. The sentimental image has
to be protected at all hazards. How often
has one found in biographies of distinguished
men, which are compiled under the domestic
eye or by the domestic hand, that youthful
struggles with sordid poverty or suffering,
that irregular experiences of budding man-
hood are ignored or half told from a mis-
guided fear of disturbing the sentimental
bias. I may not reveal the secrets of my
own prison-house. But I could recall many
a surprising example of domestic anxiety to
gloss over or misrepresent truthful and perti-
nent details in careers of immediate ancestors,
because domestic illusion, which is often bred
of the blindest conventions of propriety,

scents an unedifying savour in facts which are quite harmless but quite necessary.

Domestic sentimentality has been known to exert pressure on the biographer who stands outside the domestic circle. He at times lacks the nerve to resist all its assaults. The peril is indeed ubiquitous. It is perhaps some consolation that Shakespeare's life was written after all his descendants were dead; for who knows, had they been alive, that such a detail as that his father was a village shopkeeper and went bankrupt would have been dismissed to oblivion by an invertebrate and conciliatory biographer, at the call of an ill-balanced domestic pride.

VII

Leslie Stephen said of a recent biography —which enjoyed some vogue—that it was "too long and too idolatrous." Those epithets "too long and too idolatrous" indicate the two worst faults in biographic method, which Plutarch's teaching condemns. Of the biographic vice of idolatry, which springs largely from domestic partiality, I have already spoken enough. The vice of undue length is equally widespread and its prevalence stands in little need of illustration. It is a failing against which Plutarch's example warns us even more loudly than against idolatry. Yet it flourishes luxuriantly in spite of the master's warning. The lineal measurement of biography has no single, fixed scale. There is a threefold graduation answering in the first place to the importance of the career, in the second place to the gross amount of available material, and in the third place to the intrinsic value or biographic pertinence of the surviving records. The correspondence or the journals or the reports of conversation out of which the biographic web is to be woven vary immensely in biographic service. Lack of the raw material would make it impossible to write a life of Shakespeare of the same length as Lord Morley's *Life of Gladstone*. But brevity may be enjoined, in the case of men of the first eminence, not

solely on the ground that the raw material
is scanty. Even where the raw material be
abundant, it may be deficient in the quality
which illumines personality and may prove
useless for biographic purposes. Among
men of action especially, the faculty of self-
expression in letters and papers is often
crude and ill-developed. Diaries are filled
with formalities of daily experience, with
excerpts from travellers' guidebooks, or with
commonplace reflections. The intrinsic interest for the biographer amounts to little
more than proof of the writer's inability to
transmit his individuality through his pen.
Here drastic summarizing is alone permissible. In citing diaries the half or much less
than half is very frequently more valuable
than the whole. Rigid selection and lavish
rejection of available records are processes
which the biographer has often to practise
in the sternest temper.

It may be needful for the biographer
to examine mountainous masses of manu-
script, but he must sift their contents in

the light of true biographic principles. The balance has to be kept even between what precedes and what follows. No digression is permissible from the straight path of the hero's personality. The mode of work, which was adopted by one of the most skilful artists in black and white of our time, Phil May, may well offer the biographer suggestion here. Phil May in his drawings presented character with admirable fidelity. In the finished result the fewest possible lines were present. But the preliminary draft was, I understand, crowded with lines, the majority of which were erased by the artist before his work left his hand. Let the biographer note down every detail in fulness and at length. But before offering his labour to the world, let him excise every detail that does not make for graphic portrayal of character and exploit. No mere impressionist sketch satisfies the conditions of adequate biography. But personality is not transmitted on the biographic canvas through over-crowded detail. More than ever at the present day is there

imperative need of winnowing biographic
information, of dismissing the voluminous
chaff while conserving the grain. The grow-
ing habit of ephemeral publicity, the methods
of reporting the minutiae of prominent
people's daily life, not merely by aid of the
printing press, but by the new mechanical
inventions of photograph, phonograph and
even cinematograph, all accumulate raw
biographic material in giant heaps at an unprecedented rate. The biographer's labours
will hereafter be immensely increased; but
they will be labours lost, unless principles of
discrimination be rigorously applied.

VIII

A discriminating brevity is a law of the
right biographic method—a brevity graduated
by considerations on the one hand of the
genuine importance of the theme or career,
and on the other of the genuine value and
interest of the available material. Instances

of biographic failure, owing to infringements of this law of brevity, are legion, and one or other recent examples will leap to the minds of everyone who subscribes to a circulating library. But every law is liable in uncovenanted conditions to a temporary suspense. To every rule there are exceptions, which prove its normal justness. The longest biography in the English language is also the best. Boswell's *Life of Johnson* is indeed reckoned the best specimen of biography that has yet been written in any tongue. Critics agree that life on a desert island would be tolerable with Boswell's biographic work for companion. That verdict may be a metaphorical flight. But it has not been risked in comment on any other biography, and only in comment on two other books in English, the English Bible and Shakespeare.

To what is attributable Boswell's unique triumph, in spite of its challenge of the law of biographic brevity? The triumph is primarily due to an unexampled confluence of two very unusual phenomena. A biographic theme of unprecedented breadth and energy found biographic treatment of an abnormally microscopic intensity. The outcome is what men of science might well call a "sport."

There is no precise parallel to the episode of which Boswell's biography was bred. Dr Johnson, a being of rare intellectual and moral manliness, draws to himself, when well advanced in years, the loyal and unquestioning adoration of a rarely inquisitive young man, whose chief virtues are those of the faithful hound. Boswell's personality, save in his aspect of biographer, deserves small respect. Self-indulgent, libidinous, drunken, vain, he develops in relation to Johnson a parasitical temper which makes him glorious. Boswell pursues Johnson for twenty years like his shadow, and takes note of all that fell from the great man's lips, the tones of his voice, the expressions of his countenance. It is fortunate for us that he should have done much which self-respecting persons would scorn to do. The salt of Boswell's biography is his literal reports of Johnson's conversation, reports in the spirit of the interviewer, which run to enormous length and account for the colossal dimensions of the book.

No other biographer has sought or obtained the like opportunity of interviewing his hero and reporting his conversation. It is doubtful if any hero save Johnson could have come through the ordeal satisfactorily. It is fallacious to suggest that a mediocrity would, if submitted to the pertinacious scrutiny of a Boswell, give occasion for a biographic *tour de force* comparable with Johnson's life. There was a singular union of two exceptional human forces which, despite dissimilarity, proved to be mutually complementary. That miracle is responsible for the supreme effect. Until such a conjunction be repeated, Boswell's work will stand alone, quite out of the sphere of normal biography.

Boswell's book defies all traditional

biographic scale ; its flood of reported talk
is biographic license, not law. Yet it is
the paradoxical truth that Boswell's work
illustrates to perfection many features of
first importance to right biographic method.
In spite of its unconscionable length and
diffuseness, Boswell's biography always keeps
with admirable tenacity to the fundamental
purpose of transmitting personality. Every
page makes its contribution to this single
end. There are no digressions, no super-
fluities, no distracting issues. All the meti-
culous detail makes for a unity on which
Plutarch could hardly improve.

In the second place Boswell is the
supreme champion of the great principle
of biographic frankness ; his native candour
robs his tendency to idolatry of its familiar
mischiefs. He declines to suppress anything
that helps his reader to realize Johnson's
personality. He   bluntly   refused   Miss
Hannah More's request "to mitigate some
of the asperities of our most revered and
departed friend." He would "not cut off the

doctor's claws nor make his tiger a cat to please anybody." He was so faithful to the biographic law of candour that the frequent snubs which the doctor administered to the writer himself find a due place in the record.

Boswell's presentation of himself in the biography offers a third piece of valuable instruction to the biographer. It was not in Boswell's nature to efface himself. Yet it cannot be said of him, as of some other biographers, that he brings himself on the stage at the expense of his subject. There are biographies which fail helplessly because the writer is always thinking as much, or perhaps more, of himself than of his theme. He is seeking to share in the honours of publicity. Boswell does not efface himself, but he envelops himself in the spirit of his theme ; he stands in its shadow and never in its light.

Lastly Boswell was an industrious collector of information. It may be objected that for the fifty-four years of Johnson's life, which preceded Boswell's introduction to him, something more than Boswell knew has come to light since he wrote. It may be admitted that Boswell neglected a few sources of information from petty personal grudges against those who controlled them. The cry has indeed been lately raised, that some pigmy contemporary biographers of Johnson reveal a few phases of the doctor's character which Boswell either wilfully or unwittingly overlooked or minimised. Spots have been detected in the sun, but the sun's rays are undimmed. Boswell's achievement glows with a steadier and more expansive radiance than any other star in the biographic firmament.

There is yet another biography in the English language which transgresses·the law of brevity without marring its effect, nay, with enhancement of its effect. There is a second exception to the principle of brevity which fails to impugn the normal rule, if on grounds quite different from those which Boswell pleads with security. Lockhart's *Life of Scott* is the second best biography in the language, Boswell's biography being the first. But Lockhart's merit is mainly due to the excellence and the abundance of the raw material provided for him in Scott's ample journals and correspondence. He was spared Boswell's toil of reporter and collector of information; almost all was ready to his hands and he had merely to apply to his vast store those faculties of selection and arrangement which came of his literary efficiency and experience. It is very rare for a man of Sir Walter Scott's supreme genius, whose career and character, too, are free of dark places or mysteries prompting suppression or extenuation, to leave to a competent biographer an immense mass of fit biographic records penned by his own hand. So happy an event seems as unlikely to recur as a second meeting of a Johnson with a Boswell. Lockhart's challenge of the law of brevity is justified, and the justification barely touches normal experience.

IX

Encyclopaedic or collective biography is a special branch of biography which has not been infrequently practised, both in classical and modern times. To collective biography, in the form of national biography, Leslie Stephen dedicated immense energy, and to it I, in succession to him, have devoted almost all my adult life. The methods of collective or national biography clearly differ from those of individual biography in literary design and in the opportunity which is offered of literary embellishment. But there are points at which the method of the two biographic kinds converge. Collective or national biography, which brings a long series of lives within the confines of a single literary scheme, presses the obligations of brevity and conciseness to limits which individual or independent biography is not required to respect. Facts and dates loom larger in collective or national biography

than in other biographic forms. The object
of national as of all collective biography is
Priestley's object in scientific exposition—"to
comprise as much knowledge as possible in
the smallest compass." Indulgence in rhetoric,
voluble enthusiasm, emotion, loquacious
sentiment is for the national biographer
the deadliest of sins. Yet his method will
be of small avail if he be unable to arrange
his bare facts and dates so as to indicate
graphically the precise character of the
personality and of the achievement with which
he is dealing,—if he fail to suggest the
peculiar interest of the personality and the
achievement by some happy epithet or brief
touch of criticism. There are instances in
which a miniature memoir thus graced has
given a reader a sense of satisfaction almost
as great as any that a largely planned biography can give—the feeling, namely, that
to him is imparted all the information for
which his commemorative instinct craves.

The methods of national biography are
Spartan methods heartlessly enforced by

an editor's vigilance. It might perhaps be doubted if any of the Spartan methods of collective biography could be adopted with advantage by independent biographers who are free of the collective biographer's shackles.

Yet the virtue of liberty may be overvalued. The collective biographer submits from the outset to a strict discipline. Without under-rating the dissimilarity of the conditions in which the independent biographer works, one may often impute to him without injustice a lack of any such training as is required of his humbler brother-craftsmen. In the absence of disciplinary control, an un-trained biographer has been known to fling before his readers a confused mass of irrelevant and inaccurate information, to load his page with unimpressive sentiment, with the result that the hero's really eminent achievements and distinctive characteristics are buried under the dust and ashes of special pleading, commonplace gossip and helpless eulogy. Occasionally at any rate nothing would be lost by an exchange of a shapeless and woolly effigy from the unchartered workshop of a free and independent biographer, for a skeleton of facts and dates from the collective biographer's law-ridden factory.

X

None the less, from the purely literary point of view, a contribution to collective biography however useful and efficient cannot rank with a thoroughly workmanlike effort in individual biography. It is individual biography which gives unrestricted opportunities of literary skill. Where the theme is fit, the independent biographer has scope for the exercise of almost every literary gift.

Varied qualities are demanded of the successful biographer. He must have the patience to sift dust heaps of written or printed papers. He must have the insight to interpret what he has sifted, and the capacity to give form to the essence of his findings. A Frenchman has said that the features of Alexander ought only to be preserved by the chisel of Apelles. The admonition implies that magnitude in a career demands corresponding eminence in the biographer. No doubt the ideal partnership is there indicated. But like all counsels of perfection, this ideal union shrinks from realization. Did the precept prevail, the field of biography would be very circumscribed and few biographers would find employment. It is more workaday counsel to bid the biographer avoid unfit themes and to treat fit themes with scrupulous accuracy, with perfect frankness, with discriminating sympathy and with resolute brevity. Not otherwise is one of ordinary clay likely to minister worthily to the commemorative instinct of his fellow men and to transmit to an after-age a memorable personality.

www.ingramcontent.com/pod-product-compliance
Ingram Content Group UK Ltd.
Pitfield, Milton Keynes, MK11 3LW, UK
UKHW042149280225
455719UK00001B/204

9 781107 660908